T0146879

Spirit

The Kingdom of God Is Not in Word, but in Power

1 Corinthians 4:20

Water

The Kingdom of God Is Within You

Luke 17:21

Joseph Thomas

iUniverse®

THE KINGDOM OF GOD IS NOT IN WORD, BUT IN POWER—THE KINGDOM OF GOD IS WITHIN YOU

The Authorized (King James) Version of the Bible ("the KJV"), the rights in which are vested in the Crown's patentee, Cambridge University Press.

iUniverse books may be ordered through booksellers or by contacting:

iUniverse
1663 Liberty Drive
Bloomington, IN 47403
www.iuniverse.com
1-800-Authors (1-800-288-4677)

Because of the dynamic nature of the Internet, any web addresses or links contained in this book may have changed since publication and may no longer be valid. The views expressed in this work are solely those of the author and do not necessarily reflect the views of the publisher, and the publisher hereby disclaims any responsibility for them.

Any people depicted in stock imagery provided by Thinkstock are models, and such images are being used for illustrative purposes only. Certain stock imagery © Thinkstock.

ISBN: 978-1-5320-0341-7 (sc)
ISBN: 978-1-5320-0342-4 (e)

Library of Congress Control Number: 2016913249

Print information available on the last page.

iUniverse rev. date: 09/08/2016

I want to thank my spouse, Pam and family for keeping me in a most peaceful state taking the time while writing this book.

Walking with the Lord is very exciting learning from Him and about Him has been very unbelievable as your reading increases.

I hope you enjoy this book and tell everyone about the Kingdom of God. As you seek Him; you will find Him because He is everywhere all the time.

He (God) even wrote a book about your life before you were born. It's found in the book of Psalms. A SECRET - He will help you live and find your purpose when you're walking with Him.

I was called by The Lord in November 1976. I was Born Again in April 1977. Now forty years later I'm writing to tell all His children about Him 2016. As He told me too.

God bless you in your reading and growth.

The Author

OUR BELIEFS

There is one God manifested in three personalities: The Father, The Son and The Holy Spirit

The Bible is the mind of Christ and is the inspired, infallible and authoritative Word of God

The Reality of Satan does exist; he is called the god of the air

CHRISTIANITY IS BASED ON THE FOLLOWING
The deity of our Lord Jesus Christ His sinless life, His miracles, His vicarious and atoning death through His shed blood, His bodily resurrection, His ascension to the right hand of the Father, His personal return coming soon in power and glory as Lord of Lords and King of Kings.

Jesus said this: In the book of John 3:7, "Marvel not that I said unto thee, ye must be born again."

HERE'S SOMETHING TO THINK ABOUT Some really nice people live and impress us in our lives. Then something happens and they pass on. We hear about it and can't believe that they're not here anymore. I always ask myself, did they know Jesus? Going through this life is one thing, but when you go into the next life without Him, well it's not what I want to think about. But you and I have an opportunity to make things right for us.

For the kingdom of God *is* not in word,
but in power. 1Corinthians 4:20

The kingdom of God is within you. Luke 17:21

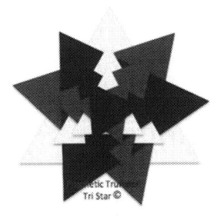

Jesus is the bright and morning Star – 3n1

CONTENTS

In writing this book, some people who do not know what the truth is. Jesus said, in the book of John 14:6, *I am the way, the truth, and the life.* He is truth, He will tell you the truth, believe Him.

I write this book to all peoples for it is written here in the book of Mark Go ye into all the world, and preach the gospel to every creature. He that believeth and is baptized shall be saved; but he that believeth not shall be damned. And these signs shall follow them that believe; In my name shall they cast out devils; they shall speak with new tongues; They shall take up serpents; and if they drink any deadly thing, it shall not hurt them; they shall lay hands on the sick, and they shall recover. Mark 16:15-18

One of my favorite verses is taken from Mark 9:23. *Jesus said unto him, If thou canst believe, all things are possible to him that believeth.*

Chapter 1

BLESSINGS FROM THE CREATOR

It says in the following scriptures to listen: "hearken diligently unto the voice of the Lord."

How many blessings can you count for your life in this next chapter below?

Taken from Deuteronomy 28:1-14 there are 31 blessings

All These Blessings Shall Come On Thee, And Overtake Thee, If Thou Shalt Hearken Unto The Voice Of The LORD Thy God.

Look What Happens Walking With God In These Two True Stories

Let's start off with a young man's life.

He met the Lord when he was five years old he said. At the age of eight teen, he graduated from high school. By the time he turned 25 he had accomplished a lot. I have learned a lot from him of Gods' Word the Bible.

He met his wife. The Lord has blessed him out of his socks. He and his wife drive new cars, 2015 truck, built a new house, filled with new furniture and much more.

He has a new motorcycle, boat and any desire that God has in store for him. All this is called the abundant Life by the hand of God.

Everyone loves this guy, mostly because he is kind and a Godly person around others. He and wife are so blessed. He's gifted with people skills.

God worked in someone else's life

A guy and his wife were looking for a house to buy in 1992. Hearing the Lord, "go east and search north-east from where you're living."

He and his wife were driving in their car. He turned left onto this street and there was a For-Sale sign at the first house on the right. He said to his wife, honey look there's a nice house, want to take a look at it? Sure she said.

He had no job at that time, his credit was way down. But guess what? the Lord promised you and I an abundant life.

They made arrangements with the real estate agent, moved in on a lease to purchase. Lived there for 24 years. The Lord blessed them as the years went by; with a new roof, new furnace w/air, new carpet, garage door, front door, water heater, new driveway and much more.

This is what the Lord can do for you hooking up with Him, be blessed. In the book of John of the Bible; John

10:10; Jesus said: "I am come that they might have life, and that they might have it more abundantly."

<u>*Who? Born Again Believers!*</u> *Coming Up!*

The Lord God Has Blessings For You!

1. God will set thee on high above all nations of the earth

2. Blessed *shalt* thou *be* in the city

3. Blessed *shalt* thou *be* in the field

4. Blessed *shall be* in the fruit of thy body

5. The fruit of thy ground

6. The fruit of thy cattle

7. Increase of thy kine (cows or cattle)

8. Blessed be the flocks of thy sheep

9. Blessed *shall be* thy basket

10. Blessed be thy store

11. Blessed *shalt* thou *be* when thou comest in

12. Enemies that rise up against thee to be smitten before thy face

13. They shall come out against thee one way, and flee before thee seven ways

14. The LORD shall command the blessing upon thee in thy storehouses

15. In all that thou settest thine hand unto

16. He shall bless thee in the land which the LORD thy God giveth thee

17. Establish thee an holy people unto himself

18. People of the earth shall see that thou art called by the name of the LORD

19. They shall be afraid of thee

20. The LORD shall make thee plenteous in goods

21. The fruit of thy body

22. The fruit of thy cattle

23. In the fruit of thy ground

24. The LORD shall open unto thee His good treasure (Spiritual Manifestations)

25. Heaven to give the rain unto thy land in His season

26. Bless all the work of thine hand

27. Thou shalt lend unto many nations

28. Thou shalt not borrow

29. The Lord shall make thee the head, and not the tail

30. Thou shalt be above only (Heaven)

31. Thou shalt not be beneath (hell)

If thou hearken (pay attention) unto the commandments of the LORD thy God which I command thee this day to observe and to do *them*.

There are 30 sum blessings in the above scriptures that may seem a little to much for someone to do for you. Of course if God can create the Sun, Moon, all the Planets and sprinkle out billions of stars, could He take care of some promises to you? I know He can, my friend. That's the good news to you.

It takes some time to learn His Voice. It took me 624 hours to know His soft-spoken voice.

Here's how to know when He speaks and gives out some wisdom to you when you hear His voice.

But the wisdom that is from above is first pure, then peaceable, gentle, and easy to be entreated, full of mercy and good fruits, without partiality, and without hypocrisy. James 3:17

Listen don't believe it when someone says to you that you can't change in life. Oh yes you can.

God wants to change you from the Adam nature to His Son's likeness, His spiritual nature. Just try to pay attention to Him and let God have His way in your life and see the wonders of Heaven come forth for you.

I counted 31 blessings that could have made a big difference in my life, if I had known these things when I was young like you are today. I'm a very rich person in Jesus Christ today.

I just wanted to share some of my riches with you so you'll have a chance to shape your life in ways you might not have had if this wisdom wasn't shared with you. God bless you.

If you want to enter into a higher walk with the Lord, just speak good words to others and say good things about your life. Words of life spoken, is like planting the seeds of a beautiful flower garden before you. They will grow and be an enjoyment to you in your life. That is exactly what the Lord is trying to tell you, coming in unto higher ground for your life. The power of life is upon your tongue; it can be life to you or death to you. What comes to you in life is what you plant (sow) in life. Yes, even in the words and actions of things we say and do.

You'll read about the farmer whom I saw in a vision. You will come to understand the neat things that the Lord has for you to plant and reap some riches of your doings.

You might learn to understand how to be very creative in life in this next chapter. Be blessed. We all need to come up to higher ground. Just like finishing one grade and going onto the next. With the Lord it's the same way. Growing up in His wisdom, gaining knowledge.

Let me say this about the Old Testament and the New Testament.

First off, the Old Testament is a shadow of things to come in today's living. And the New Testament is the substance of the things hoped for from the Old Testament. It works like this.

The blessings you are about to read are from Deuteronomy, the fourth book in the Bible. Looking at Chapter 28:1-14, there are thirty one or two blessings, and in case you don't have a farm, or some other things the words speak about here, well you will pick up these promises in the New Testament, such as. 2 Corinthians 1:20 For all the promises of God in him *are* yea, and in him Amen, unto the glory of God by us. Or in Philippians 4:13; it says: I can do all things through Christ which strengtheneth me. Brings in promises.

You see, in the New Testament we can be more creative in different ways than those in the Old Testament. Not everyone could walk with God and be a priest in the Old Testament, but now we can do things greater than those days. I hope you can come to understand what I am talking about to see the differences as well as the similarities.

Jesus said, in the book of John 10:10: The thief cometh not, but for to steal, and to kill, and to destroy: I am come that they might have life, and that they might have *it* more **abundantly**. More promises to you and me.

Actually, greater things are available to us today in the New Testament than ever before.

If we only knew how awesome the Lord God really is. Everything that has been invented, designed, including anything in warfare, discoveries in medicine and everything man has brought forth was planted in us to bring it forth in our lives. God himself placed it there while we were in our mother's womb. It is in the book written about our lives.

You see, He is the great engineer of all things. He placed things in you that will come forth but some of you won't give Him any attention in your life, so He cannot work toward that which He planted in you.

Therefore, that which He designed you for, your purpose in this life, is to glorify Him for what He placed there before you were born. The Book says we are fearfully and wonderfully made. Find your purpose in life and you'll do very well.

Wow, sometimes His Word just takes me so far into the depths of my heart and places it in His hands to let me see things I never thought of before in my life.

Matthew 13:35; I will utter things which have been kept secret from the foundation of the world.

Chapter 2

CAN WE CREATE AS GOD DOES?

Well, yes we can. In Genesis 2:26-27, *"And God said, Let us make man in our image, after our likeness: and let them have dominion over the fish of the sea, and over the fowl of the air, and over the cattle, and over all the earth, and over every creeping thing that creepeth upon the earth. So God created man in his own image, in the image of God created he him; male and female created he them."*

It works like this: when the Lord speaks to you and you're obedient in hearing His voice, what was spoken to you will come into being. That is how God creates through you or by you.

Having Jesus live in your heart means the person of faith is there also. He takes your faith you have for Him and creates whatever is His will to be done at that present time.

He will create through you according to His will.

I was sitting with my wife one morning in prayer. Here is what the Lord placed in my mind. A friend of someone close to me made a throw-over winter blanket. It is really quite beautiful. I was thinking about the blanket in the manner which the Lord had shown me. There was much needlework that had been sown into this blanket. It was made stitch by stitch until it was done. It came forth as a beautiful blanket in blue, dark blue, with yellow tones and a few other colors.

In a way, this is the same for Life. We're created in the very image and likeness of God almighty. God has given us a voice as He has Himself. When He speaks He can't help but create. We make a sound of words to create for ourselves. Oh yes we do. We haven't been taught this way yet but we can learn about speaking words.

Be not deceived; God is not mocked: for what so-ever a man soweth (speaks) in word or deed (doing with our lives) that shall he also reap. For he that soweth to his flesh shall of the flesh reap corruption; but he that soweth to the Spirit shall of the Spirit reap life everlasting. Galatians. 6:7,8.

Imagine putting away gossip, bad words, and speaking good and pleasant things in your life, and good things toward others, too. You'll read more about this in a story later.

But as we sow with words or sew with a needle and thread we'll bring forth things in our lives in the days ahead. God is there for us to bring about those things of which we have spoken, just like He has in His creation of things He speaks and creates. Remember we're created in the image and likeness of God.

Also: In Matthew 12:37, *For by thy words thou shalt be justified, (made righteous) and by thy words thou shalt be condemned.* *(Oh Oh)*

Death and life are in the power of the tongue: and they that love it shall eat the fruit thereof. Proverbs 18:21

Your words are constantly creating your life for you. Speak words of life and say good things to get the blessings of God to flow for you.

A wise son heareth his father's instruction: but a scorner heareth not rebuke.

A man shall eat good by the fruit of his mouth: but the soul of the transgressors shall eat violence.

He that keepeth his mouth keepeth his life: but he that openeth wide his lips shall have destruction. Proverbs 13:1-3

The most powerful place one too come to is: **The Kingdom of God is In Jesus' hands.** Lets take a **look at Ezekiel 37:1-10**

The Kingdom of God is very hard to grow in, or grow too, to become, like Jesus etc.

Ezekiel 37:1-10
¹The hand of the LORD was upon me, and carried me out in the spirit of the LORD, and set me down in the midst of the valley which *was* full of bones, ²And caused me to

pass by them round about: and, behold, *there were* very many in the open valley; and, lo, *they were* very dry. ³And he said unto me, Son of man, can these bones live? And I answered, O Lord GOD, thou knowest. ⁴Again he said unto me, Prophesy upon these bones, and say unto them, O ye dry bones, hear the word of the LORD. ⁵Thus saith the Lord GOD unto these bones; Behold, I will cause breath to enter into you, and ye shall live: ⁶And I will lay sinews upon you, and will bring up flesh upon you, and cover you with skin, and put breath in you, and ye shall live; and ye shall know that I *am* the LORD. ⁷So I prophesied as I was commanded: and as I prophesied, there was a noise, and behold a shaking, and the bones came together, bone to his bone. ⁸And when I beheld, lo, the sinews and the flesh came up upon them, and the skin covered them above: but *there was* no breath in them. ⁹Then said he unto me, Prophesy unto the wind, prophesy, son of man, and say to the wind, Thus saith the Lord GOD; Come from the four winds, O breath, and breathe upon these slain, that they may live. ¹⁰So I prophesied as he commanded me, and the breath came into them, and they lived, and stood up upon their feet, an exceeding great army.

There are a couple of verses that you might not recognize when Jesus spoke, it was in the Kingdom of God and it was in this Power it talks about in the scripture of: 1 Corinthians 4:20, The Kingdom of God is not in Word but in Power.

This is the most powerful verse I've found that there is.

Wouldn't you want to speak with power that the words you speak bring things into being the way they were spoken? Well, you would have to grow to that height and have the Lord speak through you to bring those Words into a power union with what the Lord would want to do.

Here is the Kingdom of God happening right now in 2016.

In the beginning of this year when January rolled in 2016, here another story to confirm its working for today.

A 14 YEAR OLD BOY DROWNS –

DEAD OVER AN HOUR & LIVES

A suburban teenager who slipped through an icy lake in January 2016 and had no pulse for nearly 45 minutes after he was rescued has made a "miraculous" recovery, doctors said. In fact, the 14-year-olds health has improved so much since the Jan. 2016 accident that doctors allowed him to go home Wednesday, was reported. "I knew there were a lot of people in my corner praying for me," an eighth-grader told the station. The teenager and two friends were walking over ice-covered Lake when the trio fell through. One of the teens managed to swim back to shore while another clung to ice. By the time paramedics arrived, the teenager had been submerged for more than **15 minutes**. Crews attempted CPR for **15 minutes** before doctors at the Hospital continued the procedure for **another 27 minutes**, reported. During that time, he showed no signs of life. But just then, the teen's mother entered the trauma room and started praying loudly, said a Doctor. "Within a matter of a **minute or two**, the teenager's heart started again." The 5-foot-3 teen's body temperature was at 88 degrees, and doctors were still worried that he could die within days if not hours. But not only did he survive — his brain functions returned to normal. "The only factors medically that were really in teen's favor is that this was a cold-water drowning," A well known Doctor told the station. Still, doctors remain baffled that his brain function was preserved. The tenacious teen, who loves playing basketball, must undergo several weeks of outpatient therapy after his brush with death. But Doctor said the teenager's recovery remains like nothing he has ever seen: "It's a bonafide miracle."

THE KINGDOM OF GOD IS MOMS FAITH AT WORK

SHE WAS OBEDIENT TO THE HOLY SPIRIT

THE SAME AS IT WAS IN: EZEKIEL 37:1-10

Chapter 3

NOW FAITH IS WHAT

Paul said, in 1 Corinthians 2:2-13

²For I determined not to know any-thing among you, save Jesus Christ, and him crucified. ³And I was with you in weakness, and in fear, and in much trembling. ⁴And my speech and my preaching were not in persuasive words of wisdom, but in demonstration of the Spirit and of power: ⁵that your faith should not stand in the wisdom of men but in the power of God.

⁶We speak wisdom, however, among them that are full grown: yet a wisdom not of this world, nor of the rulers of this world, who are coming to nought: ⁷*but we speak God's wisdom in a mystery, even the wisdom that hath been hidden, which God fore ordained before the worlds unto our glory:* ⁸which none of the rulers of this world hath known: for had they known it, they would not have crucified the Lord of glory: ⁹but as it is written,

> Things which eye saw not, and ear heard not, and *which* entered not into the heart of man, whatsoever things God prepared for them that love him.

¹⁰But unto us God revealed *them* through the Spirit: for the Spirit searcheth all things, yea, the deep things of

God. ¹¹For who among men knoweth the things of a man, save the spirit of the man, which is in him? even so the things of God none knoweth, save the Spirit of God. *¹²But we received, not the spirit of the world, but the spirit which is from God; that we might know the things that were freely given to us of God.* ¹³Which things also we speak, not in words which man's wisdom teacheth, but which the Spirit teacheth; combining spiritual things with **spiritual words.**

What actually dictates the separation of you from the Lord? It is unbelief. Unbelief only exists because you don't know Him. By not knowing Him, you don't believe in Him. I want to bring you right into His hand so you can take it and learn to walk with Him while you're living here on Planet Earth.

The natural law of God is found within the Ten Commandments. They are still in place today to obey. But, trust in Jesus by faith is the way of the New Testament.

But, there is another law called a spiritual law. For the law of the Spirit of life in Christ Jesus hath made me free from the law of sin and death. For what the law could not do, in that it was weak through the flesh, God sending his own Son in the likeness of sinful flesh, and for sin, condemned sin in the flesh: That the righteousness of the law might be fulfilled in us, who walk not after the flesh, but after the Spirit, the freedoms we cherish. Romans 8:2-4

I had to learn to accept the things I can't see because the Lord is not visible to me through my eyes. It's difficult at first but as you learn, you will understand to just trust in Him. He shows up and makes Himself known to you. Faith at work is just committing in your heart and mind after you talk with Him. Then sit back and watch things come into being that only God can bring in or do. Just believe it.

Now here is a great secret I want to share with you. In the Bible, in the book of Hebrews 11:1, it says: *Now faith is the substance of things hoped for, the evidence of things not seen.*

The substance is the person of Jesus Christ. He is the person of faith. It doesn't get any better than that. Look it up in the Greek language and it will be revealed to you.

Now as time passed by and I sat in countless church services, I came to know a little more. I grew in the knowledge of the Lord Jesus Christ as to be His partner in life.

When you have the Creator in life walking with you, you'll be someone powerful. He will use you and you'll be so blessed by the Holy Spirit.

Chapter 4

God said: "GO TELL ALL MY CHILDREN ABOUT ME"

You're reading this book to learn about how to find the way of getting God's blessings and spiritual power!

You won't believe it but you are the leaders of tomorrow! There is so much room for you at the top! Why not have the creator of life work with you as you find your purpose in life?

Just believe in yourself—put the Lord God in your heart to be with you throughout your Life.

God is so real; denying Him would be ridiculous. It would be like denying you exist, like you're not here.

Within this book is written with a great desire from the heart of the Lord for you to know Him. He continuously reaches out to all children and adults with the truth. God left an empty space in us that needs to be filled with His light, so fill it or you'll be in eternal darkness. A person will become what they give into. He gave us free will to live however we wished. He knew that people's flesh is weak and you need to choose the right path using the free will He gave you. He wants us to seek Him for the power of His Light, which we need.

People don't realize how spectacular they really are in the eyes of God. We are fearfully and wonderfully made.

This booklet is for you to find the only Way, the only Truth, and the Life of God through Jesus His Son. Learn that it is for all of us in these days we're living in.

Power to overcome, power over the spiritual enemies in life, power to create, etc. My Lord, I didn't have anyone who knew about this power when I was growing up. I missed out on a lot of good wisdom to gain the knowledge that could have escalated me to great heights. To be a type of person a little more respected. Greater Power is coming to all of us. The Power is in me.

God looked down and said all things He created are good. We need to get with it and learn how to walk with Him. Yes, the Lord wants you to know Him and walk with Him, the Creator of all things in life that has been created.

Chapter 5

I HEARD HIS VOICE

The Lord spoke and I have learned that which is spoken by God cannot stand still. It must move toward the promise of that which was spoken. The Lord has shown me the way for us to go. It is the greatest favor to be shown, if you truly seek Him, you will find Him.

The Lord spoke to me as clear as a bell. He said, "*You want the increase of something in life, so give it.*" I thought, "Wow... give it." I thought again as I began reasoning with the Lord. I kept on thinking. Well, it's a good principle that keeps on working in most anything that you might want to do or try to accomplish in life. One does have to give of one's self to get there. It's called practice.

If I wanted to be a champion skier, a basketball player or to do anything really well, I would have to give it a lot of practice.

A KEY IN LIFE

Just then I heard His Voice again, "`You have an anointing, you want the increase; increase in the giving of the service in which I send you.`"

Putting into action that which you need places you in a position to go after it to obtain that which you need experience in.

But to those called by God to salvation, both Jews and Gentiles, Christ is the mighty power of God and the wonderful wisdom of God. 1 Cor. 1:24

I placed this on the front cover; He is this wonderful being; we must consume His Word to be like Him.

Kids ~ Here Is The Power! Jesus Christ: He is the Power & Wisdom of God!

I said, "Lord, You mean that if I want some-thing then I must set my heart on it with you? I would have to place myself somehow on an increase of giving and doing it and I would have it?" "**Yep**," He said. I was thinking about how the Lord had answered me right away, without any hesitation with the word, Yep.

Since it was me who heard what the Lord was saying, I did believe in what was said and I know that which I heard Him say will surely come to pass.

As I prayed and waited on the Lord to show what He wanted me to see, He began to show me things that are important in the days we're living in. Here's what He showed me.

All children are very important to Him. He wants them to know that they can be raised up before Him in the land. Wherever you are, allow Him to come into your heart and learn to hear His Voice in your heart and conscience—it will come into place. Yes, your conscience is the genuine voice of His Holy Spirit. It's called the Rhema Word.

And if you will seek Him, you will find Him as never before.

The Lord will speak to you. God wants YOU to be comforted in these days. The youth of today needs to know that there is a greater power inside of them if you invite Him in. He knows all of us. He wants to manifest His Life in YOUR LIFE.

Most people are missing out on the greatest times of their lives and don't even know it. I hope you don't miss out on having the Lord show you things by His Holy Spirit. Wow, just wait and see what He will do in your life if you give Him a chance to show you.

You can grow up in HIM and walk in The Kingdom of God too. Here is proof right out of the Bible.

¹²Verily, verily, I say unto you, He that believeth on me, the works that I do shall he do also; and greater *works* than these shall he do; because I go unto my Father. ¹³And whatsoever ye shall ask in my name, that will I do, that the Father may be glorified in the Son. ¹⁴If ye shall ask any thing in my name, I will do *it*.

Taken from the Bible, KJV; John 14:12-14

Chapter 6

THE FARMER - PLANTING & PICKING

I believe that the Lord God Almighty is getting ready to do a new thing. I believe the Lord is going to call out the children who can make themselves ready for this great and wonderful thing the Lord wants to do in you. He will use children in ways like never before. Be ready to be raised up by His Holy Spirit.

The Lord gave me this Open Vision: sowing & reaping.

It was about a farmer standing on the side of his field in the grass. He was looking out over a huge field he had just finished plowing. He had just finished planting the seed of corn in the field.

This farmer looked over at the field that was planted and looked at the rich dark soil that was before him with a smile on his face. I saw him turn to the left and he disappeared. Just then he came back and looked at the field again. Time had passed and his harvest had come in. It was different, as it had changed to fully grown, corn as high as I had ever seen; it was so rich and green. Then, the vision ended.

I asked the Lord, "What was this vision about? What does all this mean?"

The Lord spoke right back to me and said, *"That rich field is likened unto your heart...I want you to plant My good Word of the things I've written by My Spirit.* By reading the good Word and placing it in your heart, watch and see what will come forth out of your heart and the things that will happen in your life. *"Good things are of My Word!"* and of your own words, of course.

I came to Him in prayer and asked for His love to be placed there, in the field of my heart. The fruit of His Spirit of: love, joy, gentleness, goodness, and peace. Lord, thank you for my meekness, my long suffering, my faith, and my temperance.

Thank you Lord for the fruit of Your Spirit. I can represent you in my life and allow people to see you in a big way (This fruit of His Spirit is in Galatians 5:22-23).

We all must think before speaking and believe that what we say is what will bring good to us. You shall have those things that you think in your heart, speaking good things the Lord has spoken to you and it will flow unto you in a special way.

Jesus is the creator of all things. He created hell and damnation for who rejected Him, and for the wicked. The Heavenly Father is the Judge of all things and sending His Son to die for you. If you reject Him, well, He will reject those who don't accept Jesus's sacrifice for you.

In this next verse when Jesus came to die for your sins, look how He rejoiced in His suffering.

Looking unto Jesus the author and finisher of our faith; who for the joy that was set before him endured the cross, despising the shame, and is set down at the right hand of the throne of God. Hebrews 12:2

Whatever you plant inside you will come out, and if it's Godly Wisdom, the Power is there for your possession. Believe in it to receive it.

I kept talking to the Lord: give me an attitude that would make you proud of me in my life. All that is pleasing in your sight, Lord.

I know I'm going to walk in your power and in your wisdom, Lord. For, I seek you with all of my heart.

My hope is that when people meet me, they can see these things of Jesus in me, as I have allowed the planting of the Lord's Word and of the things I wanted to be like.

Today, I am writing to everyone I don't even know. I listened to the Lord and He said, "Take it to the churches; give this book to the youth." I'm so glad to do this, to encourage you as Kings' Kids today at whatever age you may be. I would like you to feel the touch of His love from Heaven above to see how wonderful He is.

When someone looks at you, what kind of a person do they see? I hope the fruit of Love is there within you.

For God is Love.

"He that loveth not knoweth not God; for God is love. In this was manifested the love of God toward us, because that God sent His only begotten Son into the world, that we might live through him. Here in is love, not that we loved God, but that he loved us, and sent his Son to be the propitiation for our sins. Beloved, if God so loved us, we ought also to love one another." 1 John 4:8-11

I hope you are kind to others. I hope you don't speak words that would disgrace you or your parents. When people hear what you say, they'll know what your parents are like. The majority of children are products of their parents. You knew that, didn't you? Or, maybe the fruit of someone you might hang out with in life has some bad manners. You'll pick it up. Be careful.

At the end of this book is a real dream. It scared me after I had the dream. People who treat others like second-class citizens will find their just reward. I hated seeing this happen to others. Oh, bullies, where will you be at the end of all your doings?

I remember the story of David and Goliath. Goliath stood and cried unto the armies of Israel, and said unto them: *Why are ye come out to set your battle in array? Am not I a Philistine, and ye servants to Saul? Choose you a man for you, and let him come down to me. If he is able to fight with me, and to kill me, then will we be your servants: but if I prevail against him, and kill him, then shall ye be our servants, and serve us.* 1Samuel 17:8-9

Goliath was over nine feet tall. "He said I dare you to send one man to fight with me!"

Imagine the belief David had in his God.

Goliath said bad things about his God and his people.

David probably prayed: Dear God, I'm not very big, God. I know you'll always take care of me. Amen.

Who are the GIANTS today in your life? An enemy you can't see. I won't mention his name. He's called the god of the air. He deceived Eve in Genesis with Adam. There is a dream I had and boy, it will show you how to overcome your giants in this whole life of ours.

MYSTERY & SECRET THINGS OF GOD

Jesus answered, Verily, verily, I say unto thee, except a man be born of water and *of* the Spirit, he cannot enter into the Kingdom of God. That which is born of the flesh is flesh; and that which is born of the Spirit is spirit. John 3:5,6

Once you're born again of the Spirit, you can **enter in** and **see** the Kingdom of God.

Chapter 7

RAISING UP SONS AND DAUGHTERS

"But this is what was spoken by the prophet Joel; And it shall come to pass in the last days, says God, That I will pour out of My Spirit on all flesh; Your sons and your daughters shall prophesy, Your young men shall see visions, Your old men shall dream dreams. And on My menservants and on my maidservants I will pour out My Spirit in those days; and they shall prophesy. I will show wonders in Heaven above and signs in the earth beneath: Blood and fire and vapor of smoke. The sun shall be turned into darkness, and the moon into blood, before the coming of the great and awesome day of the LORD. And it shall come to pass that whoever calls on the name of the LORD shall be saved." Acts 2:16-21

Learn of the "Logos" & the "Rhema"

A lot of people believe that the Bible is a nicely written book written with letters, printed in ink—so they think. Many think it's just some history book written long ago with some truths in it.

Sorry everyone: that is all wrong.

It's The Living Word Of God ~ Christ Himself ~ The Logos Is Written In Print ~ God Is Going To Prove Himself

Using Young Children, That Are Called Out To Study And To Seek Him!

Rhema is the spoken Word of God...His Voice ~ His voice comes into your heart and in your conscience. This is where His voice will come to you by the Holy Spirit.

"I love all who love me. Those who search for me will surely find me." Proverbs 8:17

The mindset that people have and what the Lord has in mind are two different things, Praise God.

Here, read this again. Imagine obeying God's Voice!

And it comes to pass, if thou shalt hearken diligently unto the voice of the LORD thy God. To observe and to do all his commandments which I command thee this day, that the LORD thy God will set thee on high above all nations of the earth: And all these blessings shall come on thee, and overtake thee, if thou shalt hearken unto the voice of the LORD thy God. Deuteronomy 28:1,2.

Scripture is God's voice in the logos (the written word) and the Rhema is God's voice spoken in you! That is why the Holy Spirit says, *"Today you must listen to his voice."* Hebrews 3:7

When children use bad words the enemy is speaking through them. We can learn three distinct voices going on in our mind: OUR THOUGHTS ~ GOD'S VOICE ~ THE ENEMY'S VOICE.

In time, if you pay attention, you'll learn who's thinking and who's talking, You, God, or the enemy. It's easy to discern. Just pay a little attention sometimes and you'll find out you have spiritual ears to hear with. I laugh when the enemy says something. It's not God's words I hear. When the enemy speaks, I take those thoughts and cast them down and say unto those things that are not of God, I bind them in Jesus' name. In the name of Jesus I cast those thoughts out of here in Jesus's name, Amen.

This is for the Children of this World. We have to seek Him and learn to speak His Word of what we have heard. The Rhema Word is what one needs to do in obedience. He speaks and it is created.

Now, should we not bring it forth? It's up to you and me to bring God's voice in accordance to His Word. God wants to bring His Word forth as the living Word; for our lives we need to allow God to show us how real He is as the Light of Christ. It might take some time to learn these things, but, so what. Learn and walk with Him.

The Lord is going to take children in these times and days that have rolled in upon us and use them for His Glory. We are going to see children bring other people to Salvation like never before, speaking life to things as though they were. When we train our ears to hear the Holy Spirit, we shall see these things just like Jesus did when He spoke things into being. Children, listen and learn how Jesus heard and then you do the same.

Jesus said; *"I can of mine own self do nothing: as I hear, I judge: and my judgment is just; because I seek not mine own will, but the will of the Father, which hath sent me."* John 5:30

He is about to bring forth Children in junior high and high school, too. God is going to show He is Great and He needs NO ONE else to help Him accomplish what He will do on earth in these coming days.

But God has chosen the foolish things of the world to put to shame the wise, and God has chosen the weak things of the world to put to shame the things which are mighty; and the base things of the world and the things which are despised God has chosen, and the things which are not, to bring to nothing the things that are, that no flesh should glory in His presence. 1 Corinthians 1:27-29

Adults in church, who are used by God, will be used to judge what is being said by the children to make sure that everything agrees with the Word of God. That's proper and good.

In the very same likeness I bring this book to you. It's hearing the Lord speak, giving me instructions for me to carry out as a servant of God. It's the same with kids to bring forth His will. Great things will be seen by their obedience.

Have you heard of Abraham? He heard the Lord speak to him.

He believed God to bring forth what he had heard into existence.

As it is written, I have made thee a father of many nations, before him whom he believed, even God, who quickeneth the dead and calleth those things, which be not as though they were. Who against hope believed in hope, that he might become the father of many nations, according to that which was spoken, so shall thy seed be? And being not weak in faith, he considered not his own body now dead, when he was about hundred years old, neither yet the deadness of Sarah's womb: He staggered not at the promise of God through unbelief; but was strong in faith, giving glory to God; And being fully persuaded that, what he had promised, he was able also to perform. Romans 4:17-21

Looking at these verses, being as loaded as they are, brings me to my knees alone.

Look at some of these verses again. Call those things, which are not as though they were.

According to that which was spoken so shall you be strong in faith. In verse 21 stated above, what He had promised He was also able to perform it.

Do not go and cry over spilled milk, so to speak. Don't allow yourself to go backwards and look at all the times you've spent missing out on sin. No. Press onto that high calling which is in the Christ Jesus and put things in front of you. You're still young and able to subdue kingdoms in this life. God is calling everyone who will pay attention in these days we're living in. He will be with you.

Now, remember this is not a name it and claim it game or program to do your will and not God's will. That will never work. I do not believe in this manner.

This book is showing you how to acquire the REAL Voice of God that will bring things to come to pass.

There is only one person in the universe that can bring spoken things into being; He is the Lord Jesus Christ. If He speaks it, you go and get the increase of that which you believe you heard Him speak. When it comes into being, it was Jesus who did it.

But now in these final days, He has spoken to us through his Son. God promised everything to the Son as an inheritance, and through the Son He made the universe and everything in it. The Son reflects God's own Glory, and everything about him represents God exactly. He sustains the universe by the mighty power of his command. Hebrews 1:2-3

If you would like to get in touch with some-thing real and quit fooling around, here is the Son of God. There are three entities in that name right there. The three entities are God the Father, God the Son, and God the Holy Spirit together.

But, we know that there is only one God the Father, who creates everything by His Son. We exist for him. And, there is only one Lord, Jesus Christ, through whom God made everything and through whom we have been given life. The Holy Spirit carries out what Jesus the Word shows what is from the Father.

However, not all Christians realize this. Some are accustomed to thinking of idols as being real. So when they eat food that has been offered to idols, they think of it as the worship of real gods, and they're weak consciences are violated. 1 Corinthians 8:6-7

The verse above which reads, "their weak consciences are violated" is a good way to keep from hearing a word from the Lord.

Don't you realize that whatever you choose to obey becomes your master? You can choose sin, which leads to death, or you can choose to obey God and receive his approval and His Life.

Know ye not, that to whom ye yield yourselves servants to obey, his servants ye are to whom ye obey; whether of sin unto death, or of obedience unto righteousness? But God be thanked, that ye were the servants of sin, but ye have obeyed from the heart that form of doctrine, which was delivered you. Being then made free from sin, ye became the servants of righteousness. I speak after the manner of men because of the infirmity of your flesh: for as ye have yielded your members servants to unclean-ness and to iniquity unto iniquity; even so now yield your members servants to righteousness unto holiness. For when ye were the servants of sin, ye were free from righteousness. What fruit had ye then in those things whereof ye are now ashamed? For the end of those things is death. But now being made free from sin, and become servants to God, ye have your fruit unto holiness, and the end everlasting life. Romans 6:16-22

There are areas that you walk in and are not able to discern yet what can happen to you. If you pray before you go and do something the Lord will watch over you if you ask Him to. In the verses above, it said that whatever you yield to, you become slaves to.

These days, I would not want to do anything that was not from the Lord. Walking according to His plans is all I care to do. I can have success. I can have safety. I can have health, too, by reading the scriptures that have been placed in this book. I hope to feed your spirit in the righteousness of God by His wonderful Word.

There are millions of people out there. I hope this book reaches some of them and changes the direction of their lives so that they turn from their ways, walking in the Holy Glory of God that is in them after they are born again. This is something you will come to learn about in a church soon, I hope.

As your journey ends in school and you begin your next step in life, know that you were made by His greatness for your good. It won't be easy and quick. It may take your entire life to fulfill what you are meant to do and be. Push on!

Every experience will prepare you for the next. Every failure will lead you to your success. You'll be tested in ways you can't imagine. But, I have confidence that you will prevail when you're ready to leave your legacy on this world. It's what life is all about.

Chapter 8

GOD'S RIGHTEOUSNESS

As I Heard - I Prophesied One Sunday Morning.

I am the Lord thy God; know I AM is in your midst, saith the Lord of Hosts. I would say unto you, My people, every time you look unto Me. I place My righteousness on you. Yea, call upon My name saith the Lord, for many names do I have. Yea call upon My name as Jehovah Jireh, for I AM thy provider, yea call upon My name as for I have many names; Jehovah Rapha: the Lord thy God is your Physician that healeth thee. Yea call upon me, as you look unto Me I shall place my rightousness upon thee; saith the Lord. End

Looking unto Jesus, He places His righteousness on us. Having His righteousness on you opens His ears to hear your prayers. Did you ever think you were good enough to have the righteousness of God come on you? Well, that's just how much He loves you. Looking unto Jesus...Wow! If you want more of the Lord, give your life to Him and you'll become the righteousness of God in Christ Jesus yourself.

Make sure that prophecy agrees with the Word of God, who is Jesus, the Logos, which is the Word of God in the Bible that came by the Rhema, the Voice of the Holy Spirit. Let's take a look and check it out.

Any kind of prophecy must agree with the Bible, God's Word. Prophecy is meant to comfort, edify and exhort, building up the body of Christ, not tearing it down in any way, shape or form. However, prophets can speak some correction.

Learn to know who is speaking and giving a prophetic message in the church. And, don't get too involved in someone going around saying things outside the church's spiritual covering.

Who was delivered for our offences, and was raised again for our justification. Therefore, being justified (made righteous) by faith, we have peace with God through our Lord Jesus Christ: But God commendeth His love toward us, in that, while we were yet sinners, Christ died for us. Much more then, being now justified (made righteous) by his blood, we shall be saved from wrath through him. **Romans 4:25 & 5:8-9**

The word-justified means, "made righteous." I see you've noticed that.

The most important thing to understand is that we are made righteous in the eyes of God Almighty as we look to Jesus. Every time you bow your heart and head to Him He places His righteousness on you so as to let the Father see His son when He looks at you. That's kind of neat isn't it? My friend, that means a lot to me.

Jesus came to forgive you and me of all bad things that we've done wrong. He loves us so much that He counted it as Joy to Him to die for you and me. Thank You, Lord Jesus!

I wish I could say that I am perfect and have never sinned. I can't, you can't, your parents can't and anyone you know can't. We are all sinners until we bring our lives into agreement with God and learn to die out to those things that hinder us from walking with Him. We will live a life of separation from Him until we start to obey Him.

Here it says:

"And be not conformed to this world: but be ye transformed by the renewing of your mind, that ye may prove what is that good, and acceptable, and perfect, will of God." Romans 12:2 Through that scripture you just read, we see that we can come into the **good** will of God, or an **acceptable** will of God, or a **perfect** will of God.

This is where you get the benefits that will be loaded up unto you. You think I'm teasing? I'm not.

As we seek God to walk doing and living our lives according to His way in truth, we have accepted His life to come upon us. It's called His righteousness.

Chapter 9

FIVE-FOLD MINISTRY

Churches today, or at least some of them, do not even believe in Apostles or Prophets. What a shame it is when you cut short His Bible. They may miss out on a lot of spiritual blessings.

Do you think that Jesus would come along and be all these things unto us and not set up the pattern for us to walk in for ourselves?

He set up the five-fold ministry: Apostles, Prophets, Evangelists, Pastors and Teachers. This is God's way of building leaders for expanding His church. His truth, like it or not, believe it or don't believe it, doesn't stop the Lord from bringing forth Apostles and Prophets, etc., or anything else that the Lord wants to do.

If it wasn't to be so, why did He write all this in the Bible? Was it just for those people in the earlier days only? My Lord, No! Look a little harder and see these wonderful truths set before all of us to see, believe and His life manifests.

Believe it! That's why He came and walked the walk, set up a pattern in His Word and left it behind for our example to walk in it ourselves, in the very same likeness as He did.

He appointed Apostles, Prophets, Evangelists, Pastors and Teachers.

Look at what He said about we who believe in Him. "Verily, verily, I say unto you, he that believeth on Me, the works that I do shall he do also; and greater works than these shall he do; because I go unto my Father. And whatsoever ye shall ask in My name, that will I do, that the Father may be glorified in the Son. If ye shall ask any thing in My name, I will do it. If ye love Me, keep my commandments. And I will pray the Father, and He shall give you another Comforter, that He may abide with you for ever." John 14:12-16

To do the things He did! My goodness, there it is! Written for you, "He that believeth in Me," Jesus said.

Look at all those mysteries and promises written here in these five verses. Can you see the richness that God has placed here for you and me? God, in His awesome Wisdom, reveals to us such power that sometimes we can't see for the looking. Our spiritual eyes have become blurred because of unbelief. Or, maybe we need to pray and ask God to train us so He'll help us to see. Maybe to see what He wants of us.

If we bring our lives into unity with Christ we can walk and do those things He did. When He speaks, YOU CAN glorify Jesus to His Father by using you. And you're in it, too. Listen to this verse. *"For all the promises of God in him are yea, and in him Amen, unto the glory of God by us.* 2 Corinthians 1:20

If God says it, that settles it. I believe in Him and I will allow Him to mold my life into the likeness of Jesus, so I can become like Him. I will do those things He did and greater things, too. I've shed many tears allowing Him to mold me and break me. It seems to me I've failed Him so many times. Yes, I have. But, it was for my good to get me to where He wanted me to be.

I want you to remember this one thing. Religion is boring to God. It's a personal relationship that He is looking for. Knowing Him, having a personal relationship with Him, is where we are to grow to that height in Him. Yes, to become like Jesus in the earth and be just like Him doing His wonderful works and walking in the fruit of His Spirit, in order to bring glory to God His Father.

Walking in the nine Fruits of the Holy Spirit will help you walk in the anointed nine gifts of the Spirit, found in 1Corinthians 12:7-11. You can find the fruit of the Spirit in Galatians 5:22; that is what the Lord wants for you. This is what glorifies the Father through His Son. And in the flow of these gifts is normally where the POWER is revealed by the Holy Spirit of God.

Plant these words in your heart. Seek to be born again and have true riches in your life! *As it is written, there is none righteous. No, not one. For all have sinned, and come short of the glory of God. Wherefore, as by one man Adam sin entered into the world, and death by sin and so death passed upon all men, for that all have sinned ~ For the wages of sin is death; but the gift of God is eternal life through Jesus Christ our Lord. God commendeth His love toward us, in that, while we were yet sinners, Christ died for us. That if thou shalt confess with thy mouth the Lord Jesus, and shalt believe in thine heart that God hath raised him from the dead, thou shalt be saved. For with the heart man believeth unto righteousness; and with the mouth confession is made unto salvation.* Romans 3:10, 3:23, 5:12, 6:23, 5:8, 10:9-10

Visit a church where they teach from the Good Word of God the Holy Bible.

I believe the Lord will prepare your heart to come into His Kingdom and you'll become born again in His Kingdom after you pray a simple prayer, coming up in the next chapter. Praise God for His wonderful salvation.

Here's what He said in the book of John. I found out what it said in the written Word of God, then said to myself, "One day as it is written so shall I be Born Again one day to come."

It's the first step everyone must take to enter into His Kingdom. If it says it, then just do it. Please remember that the Holy Spirit inspires anything and everything written in the Bible. And the manifestation will come as He shows you and as you believe in what is written in the Bible. Such a mystery! It's the main secret of God...to walk with Him. Remember this, as you read the wisdom from God's Word. You must understand, it takes a little time and effort. But, the best teacher is the Holy Spirit.

Chapter 10

YOU MUST BE BORN AGAIN

"Verily, verily, I say unto thee, except a man be born again, he cannot see the Kingdom of God. Nicodemus saith unto him, how can a man be born when he is old? Can he enter the second time into his mother's womb, and be born? Jesus answered, Verily, verily, I say unto thee, except a man be born of water and of the Spirit, he cannot enter into the Kingdom of God. That which is born of the flesh is flesh; and that which is born of the Spirit is spirit." John 3:3-6

These scriptures are so important to you, because you have to see that if Man does things his own way then tries to teach it to you, you'll miss the boat. You must walk with the Holy Spirit of God in this Life now and be led by HIM. Life would have gone by, one dies, and there it is, NOT GOD'S HEAVEN but some-where else!

I don't want any surprises when my life passes by and it's time for me to check into Heaven. I kind of want to know what to expect. Try showing up in any city and check into a motel or hotel that's really busy. Without making reservations for a room, a place to stay, the car is what you'll have. You MUST prepare for the next Life if you're going to have Eternal Bliss. Anyone want to join me?

Now, come with me and look at this verse and tell me something. Was this person allowed to stay or what?

This is taken from the book of Matthew and this is what the King had to say to this particular person. What happened to him? Go ahead and take a look for yourself. Make sure this person the King speaks to isn't going to be YOU.

In the scripture Matthew 22:1-14:

"And Jesus answered and spake unto them again by parables and said, *The Kingdom of Heaven is like unto a certain king, which made a marriage for his son, And sent forth his servants to call them that were bidden to the wedding: and they would not come. Again, he sent forth other servants, saying, Tell them which are bidden, Behold, I have prepared my dinner: my oxen and my fatlings are killed, and all things are ready: come unto the marriage. But they made light of it, and went their ways, one to his farm, another to his merchandise: And the remnant took his servants, and entreated them spitefully, and slew them. But when the king heard thereof, he was wroth: and he sent forth his armies, and destroyed those murderers, and burned up their city. Then saith he to his servants,*

The wedding is ready, but they which were bidden were not worthy. Go ye therefore into the highways, and as many as ye shall find, bid to the marriage. So those servants went out into the highways, and gathered together all as many as they found, both bad and good: and the wedding was furnished with guests. And when the king came in to see the guests, he saw there a man which had not on a wedding garment: And he saith unto him, Friend, how camest thou in hither not having a wedding garment? And he was speechless. Then said the king to the servants, Bind him hand and foot, and take him away, and cast him into outer darkness; there shall be weeping and gnashing of teeth. For many are called but few are chosen (so you need to give this book to others. Be a witness for the Lord.)

God Wants To Prepare You Today!

Don't Miss It.

Too much time has gone by for the young people coming out of elementary school, entering into junior high and high schools. Too many children are looking for something that they don't understand and they are not being told about Christianity in public schools enough because it is not allowed. Now it is! And that's where I come in.

Who can explain to the children about your Lord and Savior? He has sent someone to reach you and show you how to be saved and bring you forth, likened unto Himself in the earth.

I kept thinking, "Did everyone make it to Heaven who died when 9/11 took place?"

It was different than those who met death with Jim Jones, David Koresh, and Haley's Comet. Those people chose to believe something else and walked right into it as blind as a bat. Don't you get caught up into those kinds of beliefs?

Then said Jesus to those Jews, who believed in him, "*If ye continue in my word, then are ye my disciples indeed; and ye shall know the truth, and the truth shall make you free.*"

Today, kids want to know the truth. Most everyone wants to experience something different in his or her life. Try Jesus Christ.

There are some real legitimate things to experience these days like drugs, pot, and booze. Even dumb cigarettes.

Wait until you experience the real thing.

You haven't seen anything yet, but we want you to know about it. Keep reading.

Do you think that a murderer is in proper normal character? I tell you they are not. The days have come and gone now. God shall arise as the wickedness has been allowed and many will fall short of His standards. He will do something new. I tell you it's on its way right now.

Mothers are the best things that we all have in life. The love received by a mother is wonderful. What a high prize they are.

Some moms are just out of whack, drinking and playing around. I'm so sorry for these people and their children.

Kids can learn to help their moms. Then she can overcome her problems and she'll love you more. Today, your mom might need a little help now and then. You can help her in the area of kindness. It's called love in action. The word love is called Charity! Kitchen love, pick stuff up and put it away love, too.

My mom gave her life for her three kids. I never missed a meal and enjoyed my childhood. When I was old enough, I got a paper route. I bought myself a real nice bike. Later, I paid for my younger brother's bike, too.

After I met Jesus, I saw how wonderful He is. It changed things in my life. WOW! And, I began to experience His Life and Love He had for me. I shouted it from the rooftop. It was like that. I could not hold it back. I was so excited. I let it all out.

Soon afterwards my mom went to church and gave her life to Jesus. She was Born Again, got baptized and now she's in Heaven.

Later on my grandmother (what a sweetheart) received Jesus. I had invited her to a Christian meeting at the Convention Center, downtown. She received Jesus into her heart. Now, she's in Heaven. I thank God that I will see them both again.

Happiness is joy in your heart. You can have it too.

Do you love your parents? Of course you do. Go to work for them. Let's give them some hope. If you don't have hope and love in your home, then it's time you get the POWER OF THE LORD in your midst.

I believe that the Lord is calling all the Children in a new way. The Lord is looking for those of you who will turn your lives around and learn of Him. Follow Him in a zealous way. Grab a hold of the things of God that is in His Word, the Bible. Learn His Voice in your conscience. Experience the wonderful walk of faith in Jesus Christ.

It says in John 14:12,13: "*Verily, verily, I say unto you, He that believeth on me, the works that I do shall he do also; and greater works than these shall he do because I go unto my Father. And whatsoever ye shall ask in my name, that will I do, that the Father may be glorified in the Son.*" I wrote this again for you, it is so important to remember this scripture. You can grow to do what Jesus did too.

It's time for you to know, absolutely know, the truth and act upon it, to see the Lord move on your behalf. Age has nothing to do with it. Twelve years of age to a hundred and ten is fine with the Lord. Seek Him, and you, at whatever age, shall find Him.

If ever a time has come, now is when you should turn your life around. Take hold of God's hand in Christ Jesus and what He has for you. He's calling you onto the battleground right now. Yes, a battleground where there is a war going on in your life. You will have spiritual wars and it's okay. You can win through Christ Jesus our Lord.

It might be with your mom or dad at home. God's calling you, because SOME moms and dads didn't pay attention to the Lord in raising you. Now, the time has come for the Lord to step in and take control of Your Life if you'll come to Him and be used by Him. Maybe you don't have any problems at all. Well that is great. You are blessed.

Yes, through you, your parents can come to realize Eternal Life. Hey, mine did. He wants to use you. He wants you to realize how real He will make Himself to you if you will let Him.

Believe me. The Lord wants to fight your battles. It's the Lord's war, not yours. He will make a way far better for you and your parents. He'll give them a new life, a new hope, a new power that is only realized through Christ Jesus our Lord. Will you come?

Some friend, a church, or a school fundraiser gave you this book. They paved the way for you to come to know what millions of other kids know all around the world, and that's Jesus. I will guarantee you this one thing about the Lord. He will never let you down. If you can have patience with Him and learn about Him, He will show you His wonders.

His wonders in Heaven, His wonders in the earth, His wonders in your life, His wonders in your particular situation.

There is no failure in Jesus Christ. He is Lord over ALL THINGS! I can't always understand Him but I do know He has my best interest at hand with His heart.

When He comes again for His church, will be ready?

Here, let me say that again.

HE IS LORD OVER ALL THINGS THAT PERTAINS TO LIFE AND GODLINESS!

What is wonderful about all this is you're a human being. You are in a place to learn about what God is going to do. Want to trade places with me? I'll trade places with you if I could! If I knew what I know now, praise God.

Grace and peace be multiplied unto you through the knowledge of God, and of Jesus our Lord, According as his divine power hath given unto us all things that pertain unto life and godliness, through the knowledge of him that hath called us to glory and virtue: Whereby are given unto us exceeding great and precious promises: that by these ye might be partakers of the divine nature, having escaped the corruption that is in the world through lust. 2Peter 1:2-4

Wow, multiplied unto you through the know-ledge of God!

The more of the Bible you read, the more God will become real unto you.

God that made the world and all things therein, seeing that he is Lord of Heaven and earth, dwelleth not in temples made with hands; Neither is worshiped with men's hands, as though he needed anything, seeing He giveth to all life, and breath, and all things; and hath made of one blood all nations of men for to dwell on all the face of the earth, and hath determined the times before appointed, and the bounds of their habitation; that they should seek the Lord, if haply they might feel after him, and find him, though he be not far from every one of us. Acts 17:24-27

Now, I bring you unto those very same scriptures that found their way inside of my heart. Find a Bible and read the great Romans road.

Romans 3:10, 3:23, 5:12, 6:23, 5:8, 10:9-10.

I did a little planting of these scriptures in my heart. As I rested day and night the Lord gave the increase to me. See how He works by simply believing He will work for you, too. Study and you will learn about this.

You will begin to say, "Was that you, Lord?" Yes you will! I guarantee it!

You just read some wonderful scriptures and it will work in your life. You will be seeking Jesus because He will call you. Can you believe it? He'll be calling you and bringing you into His Kingdom. He will show you wonderful and marvelous things your eyes haven't seen before. How did I write this book if I didn't enter and see for myself?

Your next step will be to find a church where they allow the Holy Spirit to move. God is the one here to lead you and guide you into all truth for today. He points to Jesus in everything. The Holy Spirit is so very precious and gentle that you will totally love to be in His presence when you finally learn how to walk with Him.

A Total Salvation

What is total salvation for an individual?

1. The sin obligation must be paid.

2. One must be viewed by GOD as never having sinned.

3. The Law by which one is declared a sinner must be removed.

4. One will have peace with GOD.

An Explanation:

1. The Lord Jesus's body was beaten before the crucifixion; that paid for the Believer's sin debt for our transgressions (trespasses). He was bruised for our iniquities (wrong moral ways of thinking, sinning ignorantly). The chastisement (punished for us that we would have peace with God) He took so that we could have peace. By His stripes we are healed.

But he was wounded for our transgressions, he was bruised for our iniquities: the chastise-ment of our peace was upon him; and with his stripes we are healed. Isaiah 53:5

2. GOD must view the believer as having never sinned. *"Much more than being now justified by His blood, we shall be saved from wrath through Him."* Remember, "justified" means "just as if I had never sinned." Romans 5:9

3. *The Law of Sin and Death by which one is declared a sinner must be removed. Blotting out the handwriting of ordinances that was against us, which was contrary*

to us, and took it out of the way, nailing it to His cross. Colossians 2:14

4. Peace with GOD. *Therefore being justified by faith, (made righteous) we have peace with God through our Lord Jesus Christ.* Romans 5:1

Comment: The Scriptures teach us how the Lord Jesus paid, not for the Believers only, but the sin debt of every individual. The Lord Jesus paid the sin debt and GOD made the gift available to all men. The gift of eternal life is accepted by the one who believes and confesses that Jesus died for their sins.

If God is to place the Believer into the body of the Lord Jesus, the Believer must be in a condition of having never sinned. GOD does this for the believer by the blood of Lord Jesus, which washes away all sin: past, present and future. Thus, GOD views the Believer as having never sinned and can have the HOLY SPIRIT immerse (baptized) the Believer into the body of Christ.

The Law by which one is declared a sinner must be removed for the Believer. The body of Jesus nailed to the cross at Calvary accomplishes this.

You have so many rights in your Savior. It's wonderful to come in and see how it will all work for you. I see it like a big door that God is opening for you that you couldn't open before because of its size. It's going to open wide now.

Maybe, you think your size is a BIG THING. Sorry, guys and gals. You have to think when you come to Him. He becomes yours and you can't be bigger than that.

Come on into that spiritual Church where you're going to start to allow the Holy Spirit to teach you and move you to greater heights.

This is declared in Colossians 2:14: *Blotting out the handwriting of ordinances that was against us, which was contrary to us, and took it out of the way, nailing it to his cross.*

The flesh wars against the Spirit and the Spirit against the flesh. Thus, the Law must be removed. The Believer and GOD accomplished this by His Son. Knowing we have "peace with GOD" by believing in what Jesus did for us, we can have a relationship with God. If you sin and make a mistake we can have our sins taken away, past, present and future. All of our sins are washed away by the blood of Jesus.

If one is with Christ Jesus, there can be nothing other than peace with God.

One of the greatest things you can do is be Born Again. Give your Life to the Lord Jesus Christ.

Repent for your sins and accept Jesus into your heart. Turn your life over to Him and watch Him take over from day to day.

I have a cousin. He told me that he went to church and received Jesus into his heart. He was born again four different times in church services. Nothing happened to him in the things of the Lord, he told me. How many times have you been born into this world? How many moms do you have? You are born again by receiving Jesus Christ into your heart once. It is one of the greatest miracles in life of how God set this up for us. Jesus died once and for all. He won't come alive and die over and over.

I told him, "If you repented and truly asked God to forgive you and asked Jesus to come into your heart and live His life in you, then you must walk by faith!" Faith is believing in what the Bible says. You'll learn by reading the Bible. Then you can see God move in your life and watch God do marvelous things for you.

HERE IS A PRAYER OF SALVATION Read it and if you mean it with all of your heart you'll be transferred into His Kingdom spiritually.

A PRAYER OF SALVATION TO BE BORN AGAIN!

"Lord Jesus, I confess that I am a sinner; come into my heart and be Lord of my life. Take my life Lord Jesus and show me the way to live my life for you. Thank you for dying on the cross in my place of judgment for my sin. I believe you were raised from the dead for my justification, making me righteous for your sake. I believe Heaven will be my home when my time is up and I pass away to be with you. In Jesus' name I pray. Amen."

You just got **BORN AGAIN**

You must remember the date of this prayer and go and tell someone about it to prove you had believed in the action you took and prayer you prayed.

Send me an e-mail: prophet@ymail.com

You now believe you're going to go to Heaven?

Write in today's date right here:_____.

Or, on a piece of paper so you'll remember it.

This book is yours forever. You can write in it.

Therefore if any man be in Christ, he is a new creature: old things are passed away; behold, all things are become new. 2 Corinthians 5:17

If you prayed this prayer above, thank the Lord that you want to believe in it and you meant it. Showing you prayed it from your heart and believing it is putting FAITH into action before God Almighty. He sees and knows all things all the time.

HE WORKS WONDERFULLY FOR YOUR GOOD.

It all began when I prayed that prayer that you just prayed.

It started this way: I said to the Lord God, "The pastor preaches you're the same yesterday, today and forever. I believe that and because you talked to Moses way back in the Old Testament, you can talk with me right here with me today."

What happened after was the Lord taught me His voice as God, and said to me one day many many days after I receive Jesus into my life, I will be learning about His voice.

He told me to look back and count the days for two years since I had been listening to Him speak to me. He showed me that He had confirmed His voice to me so many times.

I believe that I counted about 624 hours of hearing and learning His voice. Two hours a day at church, I went three times a week. That's six hours a week Sunday morning, Sunday night and Wednesday night. Times 52 weeks times two years equals around 624 hours.

Then the Lord told me to say the things that I had heard from Him to prophesy what I had heard from Him. At first I was frightened almost to death, but I began to feel comfort with what I had heard and what He showed me through the preaching of His Word. I was in agreement with what God had given me in the first place.

THE TRUTH SHALL SET

YOU FREE

Chapter 11

A DREAM ~ POWER OVER THE ENEMY

Flying an Airplane, I learned as the engines roared.

I remember one time early in the morning just before waking up, I was dreaming about flying this airplane. I don't know if I was the pilot or co-pilot.

This other person and I were in the cockpit. I was sitting in the seat and had noticed I was engaged in the operation of flying this airplane. Something like a steering wheel was in my hands.

The dream started like this. I heard a noise. I didn't know what it was but it was dark and I can't remember being focused with my eyes to see. I just heard noise. It was a roaring of some sort, "rrrrmrrrmmmrrrrrmmr." It was a rumbling sound, like some kind of a motor. I heard this sound over and over as I was trying to figure it out in my sleep and I just couldn't put it together. It came to me that I should ask about the rumble, so I said to myself, "What is this noise I hear? Can someone help me?" Just then, in a moment of a few seconds, it came to me that I was sitting in the cockpit of an airplane and I felt this steering wheel in my hands. I could see little lights on like the lights of the instrument panel all lit up. I noticed that I was twelve thousand feet in the air. All of a sudden it came to me that

I had to make an emergency landing. I was running out of fuel fast and I had to land this airplane.

I didn't know how to fly this airplane and I sure didn't know how to land it either. All of a sudden I learned that I had this pilot or co-pilot or someone else there with me. He was standing behind me and said in a soft-spoken voice, *"Have faith in Me for I am with you."*

It came to me as I questioned the voice who it was that had spoken those words to me. I said, "What am I doing here in this dangerous position, flying this airplane? Can I get out of here right now, please?" The soft answer was, **"No. You're going to land this airplane and trust in Me. I am with you and you can land it very easily if you listen to Me,"** the soft voice said.

It finally came to me that those soft-spoken words were from the Lord because I had heard Him speak to me many times in the past. Now I knew I could land this airplane with great assurance.

It seemed that my partner didn't pass out any orders to me. He was just there to alert me of things that I needed to know while I was flying this twin-engine plane.

God brought things to my awareness through this whole dream. How He did this was through His voice. I knew that I could give Him a one-hundred percent approval of whatever I heard from Him while flying this airplane. As for any other time in my life that I had heard from Him, it came to pass just the way He had spoken to me.

The airplane was dropping in altitude quickly and all of a sudden I saw a landing airstrip with the lights flashing so we could land. I gave my steering wheel a left hand turn and the plane headed in the direction of the lights.

As we approached the airstrip for landing, I heard the directions of everything I had to do to land and we came in safely. I don't remember calling in for directions or permission for landing. The lights appeared and then I landed. The fuel was very low and it wasn't a matter of choice. It was landed because of circumstances and because the landing strip appeared when needed.

We both got out of the airplane and all of a sudden we were surrounded by what looked like enemy soldiers. I remember looking down the barrels of those rifles that were pointed at us, as we became prisoners. I was extremely nervous.

These soldiers ushered us into a big hangar, then into a little room where the enemy interrogated us. I could not recognize what country they were from. In a strange English they said for us not to speak. We did as they told us. My patience was on the short side and a lot of time went by just waiting and waiting. One of the enemy soldiers came in and talked with another soldier for a few minutes.

They walked up to us and motioned for us to go back into the larger hangar. As we entered into the larger hangar, my eyes could not believe what I was looking at. There was the airplane in the hangar. Strangely enough it looked like paper was wrapped all around it. Little strips of paper in millions of pieces had been wound around the body, the wings, the motors and even the propellers.

What first came to me was that there would not be a way out of here and my life was going to be spent as a prisoner! I wanted to die right there on the spot as I was thinking about being held prisoner and being locked up and held in bondage. I did not want to face the rest of my life like this.

Just then, as I was in deep thought (actually these thoughts were not mine) a soft voice spoke to me again and said, **"Run up to the airplane and start ripping the paper off."**

I don't know why I was thinking this as the soft voice said it again. "Go ahead and just tear the paper off." Just then as I was walking towards the airplane, something else happened. I noticed I was loaded with **FAITH**. I knew just then that I should start doing as I had heard. I ran up to the airplane and started ripping the paper off. I don't know why, but I had all the courage that a person could have to do just about anything one wanted to do. As I was thinking everything over, I just started tearing off the paper. Then as my faith was being built up inside of me, I started hurrying like I was running from a fire or something.

I could not believe what followed. No one at the time made a move towards me as I tore the paper off of the airplane wing. My partner was watching me as I turned around to look at Him. He gave me a look of assurance that was so different than anything I could describe to you. I started ripping the paper off as fast as I could. It seemed as though I would have enough time to tear it all off with no problems.

I jumped up on the wing of the twin-engine airplane and a guard started yelling at me. He said, "Hey you, what do you think you're doing?" I didn't turn around to look at him. I was thinking, "Oh Lord God help me!" Just as fast as I had those thoughts, the soft voice spoke to me and said, "***Turn around and point your finger at him and speak to this guard with authority.***" I rose in faith and told the guard to help me with tearing off the paper. It went like this.

Just then I swung around. I was still on the wing of the airplane and I looked at the enemy in the face and said to him, "*In the name of Jesus Christ, tear this paper off of the airplane and make it fast.*"

To my surprise this dumb guard started doing just as I had commanded him to do. Just after he had started to help tear the paper off, two more guards came up to me, screaming, and said to get down right now and stop tearing of the paper off of this plane.

I turned around and my spirit was loaded with FAITH. As before, I said to these two guards, *"In the name of Jesus Christ help tear off this paper."* These dumb guards obeyed. It seemed as though minutes had run by in my dream and I looked up and said to another guard, *"Fill up the plane with fuel in the name of Jesus."* I commanded it and it was done instantly.

I could not believe the power I had in that wonderful name of Jesus.

I was flooded with Faith and the Joy was mine. I knew that the Lord God was with me and really experienced a scripture that reads like this:

"I can do all thing through Christ which strengtheneth me." Philippians 4:13

I gave one more command and that was for this guard to open the hangar doors. *"In JESUS'S name!"* I yelled at him. He obeyed, as I turned to look for my partner, the one with the soft-spoken voice: *"Come on. Let's get out of here."*

We jumped into the cockpit of the airplane, cranked up the engines. The paper that was on the propellers flew off. I pushed the handle all the way down and the engines roared to life as my heart pounded in a fury. I pushed the handle to release the brakes. It snapped into the unlock position and we started rolling as fast as possible out of the hangar.

With the engines still roaring I pushed the handle down to full blast. Out onto the airfield we went down the runway. The thrust of the engines was wonderful as we lifted up off of the ground. I felt the liftoff as we went into the air to make our escape. I had a wonderful feeling. It was Joy In My Heart!

I watched the ground pull away from us. It felt so good to know that I had just experienced a victory in my life in this dream with the Lord being right there with me all the time and somehow knowing it, but at the same time not realizing something about it yet.

This is exactly how Jesus will be there all the time with you. It's hard to believe when you can't see Him, but He will be there with you. Remember, that is if you invited Him into your heart. That's where you asked the King of Glory to be, right there in your heart.

This story goes along with some scripture. It's in the book of Luke 10:19 & 20. *"Behold, I give unto you power to tread on serpents and scorpions, and over all the power of the enemy: and nothing shall by any means hurt you. Notwithstanding in this rejoice not, that the spirits are subject unto you; but rather rejoice, because your names are written in Heaven."*

The Son of God, Jesus said this unto us. You want the power? Well, there the Holy Spirit writes it to you and me. I use it all the time.

Dreams can come true. It seemed this one did!

As I started waking up, my senses were telling me that I just had a really wonderful dream. I lay there for a while. Then I said to the Lord, "Why did I have that dream and what does it mean?"

The Lord spoke to me instantly and said, "Meditate for a minute and think of all the problems you have in your life." As I did that He spoke again. "**You have that same authority in my name. Speak to the problems.**" He showed me how to speak so when the enemy came in and attacked me, he would be defeated immediately.

Just as I had spoken to those enemy guards in the hangar in Jesus's name as He directed me, I told myself that I have the authority to do whatever I need to vanquish the invisible demons in this life.

Scripture came to my mind just then, as I was meditating and listening to whatever He would say. I wanted to hear His wonderful soft-spoken voice.

John 15:7: "**If ye abide in me and my words abide in you, ye shall ask what ye will, and it shall be done unto you.**"

You can have this same power that is in and through His name. God will cause us to triumph gloriously in His Son's name the Lord Jesus Christ. Amen.

This is what the Lord wants you to know about this dream. *"You can get the Power, too, through Jesus Christ by being born again!"*

Pilate therefore said unto him, "Art thou a king then?" Jesus answered, "**Thou sayest that I am a king. To this end was I born, and for this cause came I into the world, that I should bear witness unto the truth. Every one that is of the truth heareth my voice.**" John 18:37

This tells me that if you are walking with the Lord and seeking Him in the Bible, then you are of the truth, seeking His will.

You must see that this soft voice that I heard comes from God. He was there with me all the time and He said to trust Him and do what He said to do.

Here, this is what the Lord's voice is like. *"But the wisdom that is from above is first pure, then peaceable, gentle, and easy to be entreated, full of mercy and good fruits, without partiality, and without hypocrisy. And the fruit of righteousness is sown in peace of them that make peace."* James 3:17-18

When you learn to hear His Voice you'll know what it's like. It has some wonderful benefits to it, too. There's real life in His Voice and you can go out and collect on it. Whatever you hear Him say, when you walk in obedience and say it too, and believe it because you know God spoke it to you, it will come into being. I guarantee it.

School is a great place to get an education and church is a great place to get the spiritual wisdom of the knowledge to walk personally with the Lord Himself.

Luke 10:19 says, *"Behold, **I give unto you power** to tread on serpents and scorpions, **and over all the power of the enemy:** and nothing shall by any means hurt you."*

Use the verse above when you feel the enemy is attacking you or your loved ones, family members or friends. You've got the Power!

I wonder whom this power is given to? It is for all of us, because you now belong to Jesus. He said it so you don't get kicked around by the enemy.

There are some wonderful manifestations that
He has for you. Prepare your life for His Life.
Wow! Imagine ~ walking around with the
Creator of the Universe in you, having the power
as though you invited Him in your heart.

OUR MISSION NOW IS TO SHARE HIS LOVE TO

EVERYONE THROUGH HIS RIGHTEOUSNESS.

PRAYER + PRAISE

Say a prayer for yourself, your dad and mom, family members, as well as your pastors. Pray for this country, praise Him and go forth in life.

DELIGHT YOURSELF IN GIVING OUT HIS LOVE.

WALKING IN HIS LOVE AND SHARING IT WITH OTHERS WILL ENLARGE HIS JOY IN YOU.

HE GAVE ME THE ABOVE SENTENCE AS I WAS DRIVING ON AN INTERSTATE HIGHWAY.

HE SAID: "WHEN YOU'RE WORKING WITH ME, WALKING IN MY LOVE, YOUR JOY WILL BE FULL."

I CAN NEVER SAY ENOUGH OF HOW SUPER WONDERFUL THE LORD REALLY IS!

Here is a key! Just act like you own Jesus Christ if you said that prayer earlier and meant it.

You do own Him and He is your new boss which you're following in life to do His will.

PROPHESY

Surely I would say unto you a big huge wave is coming; it is My hand saith the Lord, and in My hand is a key that will unlock your hearts for My Glory; it will flow through those who will seek me with all their heart, saith The Lord. My Glory will cause those who come into contact with it, will be changed in a moment, yea surely the experience of its power will change those who don't know Me, and will want more of Me, saith The Lord. Keep your eyes on Me and watch for it, for it is not far off and will come in the days ahead, saith the Lord God Almighty.

Chapter 12

A VISION: THE NEXT LIFE TO COME

In this Vision I saw little stones that were so very beautiful and sparkling with all colors, shaped all differently. I knew that theses stones were very special and somehow the Lord would build a house that joined together in a perfect fit.

Each stone had many different shapes, but God knew how and where we were to fit into this beautiful house. Theses stones were clear as crystal. When the Lord came upon them they were rich in color and bright and brilliant as could possibly be. It looked something like a great big perfect diamond.

No human being has seen anything that compares with what the Lord God can show you and what He can do. This is the difference between a real flower that is so soft and beautiful and wonderfully made with a sweet scent. Compare this to a fake flower that appears to look good until you get close to it and find out there is no real scent or sweetness in its making.

It's not quite like the one you can adore and smell. See the life with real beauty that is in it.

I was in the Spirit. I looked and this is what I saw. These stones shone forth in brilliance of color and were so very beautiful to look upon.

They flowed out from a great door of doors of the New Jerusalem high up in the sky, went out into space, and flowed down to the new earth. The purpose is to set up a place where people would gather to adore God Almighty. People will come and see His children who served Him in a time when TIME was in place. Those children are the ones to be used. As these Lively Stones came and settled down on the new earth they were shaped into a house God built with them.

And His presence came upon them and filled all the lively stones that had proceeded out from the New Jerusalem. People that were there on the new earth came and bowed down unto the house that was made up of the lively stones. The Lord God came upon it and it was very bright and His Presence was very great to be felt. It is the most wonderful thing to see and it was so wonderful to feel something from the Creator. It is almost like Paul said in 2 Corinthians chapter 12; words which are unutterable at this time.

Can you see your hope, my brethren and sisters? The difference between the Godly man and woman who are overcomers and who have a relationship with God, verses the individuals who do not? There is a difference between one who goes to church and listens to the Word but never gets the abundance of the true life that is there for them versus the one who has a relationship with God Himself, and knows Him personally.

In the church when I saw the vision, praise and worship was over and I could see this house in Heaven on the New Earth. God showed me that these stones (we are called lively stones) would know where to go to set up a camp where He would manifest Himself in this house of living stones. In the Old Testament the children of Israel had a tabernacle that they carried around, and set up the tent where God would come and manifest His Glory in the Holy of Holies. A High Priest would enter into His Glory once a year.

I believe that there is going to be a separation between so-called carnal Christians because they did not pay attention to what was going on with the Lord God Almighty, which is currently called time.

Carnal Christians are separated here on earth now. So will it be the same in the next life? It's a separation between many. So shall it be with the Lord God in the next life, too.

I know that on the new earth there will be people on it. The new earth will be without any sea, the Bible says. There is going to be a new Heaven and a new earth. The New Jerusalem is going to be where God is all the time and the Living Stones are going to live in this New Jerusalem, walking on streets of gold. Here is the scripture below.

In the book of Revelation 21:1-2, it states, *"And I saw a new Heaven and a new earth: for the first Heaven and the first earth were passed away; and there was no more sea. And I John saw the holy city, New Jerusalem, coming down from God out of Heaven, prepared as a bride adorned for her husband."*

I know that some of this stuff is deep and some of it you won't understand yet. But, what I do need you to see, the wonders of God Almighty.

He has come to offer His Life to you. If you'll pick up His Word and begin to find out what's in the Bible for you, you'll become rich in spiritual things that are unbelievable.

You have one exciting Life to live when you walk in the Wisdom of the Lord. Read Proverbs about Wisdom and how rich it is.

Happy is the man that findeth wisdom and the man that understands. For the merchandise of it is better than the merchandise of silver, and the gain thereof than fine gold. She is more precious than rubies: and all the things thou canst desire are not to be compared unto her. Length of days is in her right hand; and in her left hand riches and honor. Her ways are ways of pleasantness, and all her paths are peace. Proverbs 3:13-17

As I was reading the Bible one day, I saw this same vision written in the scriptures maybe 20 some years later after I had seen that vision.

It is written: Ephesians in Chapter 3:18-22

For through him we both have access by one Spirit unto the Father. Now therefore ye are no more strangers and foreigners, but fellow citizens with the saints, and of the household of God; And are built upon the foundation of the apostles and prophets, Jesus Christ himself being the chief corner stone; In whom all the building fitly framed together groweth unto an holy temple in the Lord: In whom ye also are builded together for an habitation of God through the Spirit.

Blessings are waiting on you to receive!

Matthew 6:14-15: "*For if ye forgive men their trespasses, your Heavenly Father will also forgive you: But if ye forgive not men their trespasses, neither will your Father forgive your trespasses.*"

Chapter 13

LIFE/DEATH – RICHER/POORER

I was thinking about humans in their various religions. The Muslims, Jews and Christians. What plan should we believe in? Well mostly I believe that religion is a good thing to have and one gets to believe in something of a higher power to look up to. People get lost.

Somehow man gets snagged on that last sentence. Higher power, then greed comes along, then war comes because man wants to have all the things in life to make oneself have the best there is and rule in one's life and to be on top and get his way through life.

You see, as I look at the end of all things, it can't be based on having everything there is in life.

I want you to consider this one thing. Collect all the gold and silver that there is or could ever possibly be. Then collect all the diamonds and jewels there are and stack it all in one place. Now take North America and say you own that much land. Okay, take all the land in the whole wide world and say it's yours. Do you have enough to satisfy yourself? Will you be content in life? When the end comes, where will you be?

I'll tell you the truth—I would not accept this. There is one thing that most people miss out on. The greatest miracle in life is being born again. Being transformed into God's Kingdom. To live with the Creator and walk on streets of gold in the next life, and the beauty that's there with the Lord Jesus Christ. Wow! Miss that and you have missed it all.

The Lord gave me a dream of people falling off of the edge of a cliff. I yelled at them in the dream but they could only look over at me. It was if they had no control over what was happening to them. Please forgive everyone you have ought against. AND do good with your life. Live for the blessings at the beginning of this book, in Chapter 1. If it is written, it shall come to pass.

Let God arise, let His enemies be scat-tered: let them also that hate Him flee before him. As smoke is driven away, so drive them away: as wax melteth be-fore the fire, so let the wicked perish at the presence of God. Psalms 68:1-2

This scripture above reminds me of a scene in a movie I had seen.

"Raiders of the Lost Ark."

This next section was taken from the 700 Club, CBN TV program on Nov. 26, 2013, @ 9:00 – 10:00 AM.

Bill Wiese was a guest speaker and had an out-of-body experience. He wrote about it in his book, titled:

What Happens When I Die?

Bill Wiese talked about the Apostle Paul, as he wrote to us in the Bible, in 2 Corinthians 12:1: *It is not expedient for me doubtless to glory. I will come to visions and revelations of the Lord.* He had a Vision in an out-of-body experience.

Bill Wiese said: God withdrew His attributes from hell, in James 1:17, it says: *Every good gift and every perfect gift is from above, and cometh down from the Father of lights, with whom is no variableness, neither shadow of turning. See Bill's Video on YouTube at: 23 minutes in Hell.*

Attributes are God qualities, characteristics, traits, features, powers, properties; something to credit some body with these elements are called attributes. So saying all that means these good things of God are not down in Hell. Just all bad things.

Hell is full of darkness, because in 1John 1:5, it says: *This then is the message, which we have heard of him, and declare unto you, that God is light, and in him is no darkness at all.* And in John 1:4, *In Him was life; and the life was the light of men.*

So if God took away His attributes from hell, then there is not light, just total darkness. Not just for a little time: it's forever and ever. People don't have a right to see the light or to have any kind of fellowship.

God is love. In 1John 4:15&16, it says: *Whosoever shall confess that Jesus is the Son of God, God dwelleth in him, and he in God. And we have known and believed the love that God hath to us. God is love; and he that dwelleth in love dwelleth in God, and God in him.*

Isaiah 38:18 says this: *For the grave cannot praise thee, death cannot celebrate thee: they that go down into the pit cannot hope for thy truth.*

Bill Wiese said that in hell there are maggots, demons, fire, snakes, screaming. You can't get away from it. Screams lasting forever. There is no end.

Come on people, Jesus died a horrible death to save us from this awful place. He sent His word to save us while we still have time. It's almost like if we push the Lord aside that we might do our own thing and will have to live here in a bad place because we didn't pay attention.

You might ask how God can reject us, for He is love. If you reject Him, He will reject you. But, Jesus died a horrible death to keep us out of a horrible place. I prayed you'll be transformed from this life into His Kingdom by the earlier prayer I placed here in this book for you. I love you with the love of Jesus; that's my job to love one another. Yours too if you've joined in His Kingdom.

Trust in the LORD with all thine heart; and lean not unto thine own understanding. In all thy ways acknowledge him, and he shall direct thy paths. Be not wise in thine own eyes: fear the LORD, and depart from evil. It shall be health to thy navel, and marrow to thy bones. Proverbs 3:5-8

Prepare Your Life For The Way of The Lord!

One last thing: how do you put your faith to work so that God would respond to you? Just thank Him for what you have need of. Say it out loud to Him. He is omnipotent, (powerful everywhere). Thank you Lord; I believe you can hear me and you will show me the way through life victoriously. In Jesus's name, Amen.

Remember we're walking by FAITH now! Not by sight.

That's how you do it. Thank Him for your needs. He knew what you needed before you asked. He just wants you to look to Him in life.

This next verse reveals how I want to grow and be like Shadrach, Meshach, and Abednego. Here it mentions what it will be like when the Kingdom of God rises up.

And in the days of these kings shall the God of Heaven set up a kingdom, which shall never be destroyed: and the kingdom shall not be left to other people, but it shall break in pieces and consume all these kingdoms, and it shall stand for ever.

Guess what? This whole Kingdom is about God raising up HIS KINGDOM Of GOD. Would you like to be in it? That's what this book is about.

Learn all about JESUS and come on in.

Prophesied Empires of Kings

Babylon – head of gold kingdom
Medo-Persia – another kingdom
Greece – third kingdom of brass
Rome – the fourth kingdom iron
Europe – the feet, toes, clay, & iron and
powers of this kingdom

Then the 2nd Coming of Christ

THE KINGDOM OF GOD HAS COME

And in the days of those kings shall the God of heaven set up a kingdom which shall never be destroyed, nor shall the sovereignty thereof be left to other people; but it shall break in pieces and consume all these kingdoms, and it shall stand for ever. Forasmuch as thou sawest that a stone was cut out of the mountain without hands, and that it brake in pieces the iron, the brass, the clay, the silver, and the gold; the great God hath made known to the king what shall come to pass here after: and the dream is certain, and the interpretation thereof sure. Daniel 2:44

When you hear about the Jewish people building their new Temple, look up, for He is on His way back to take up the many who put their trust in Him.

If you read in the book of Daniel chapter 2:1-49

We are in these days of the ten toes. Jesus is in the picture at the bottom. Time is running out, so share with others to get this book. Want blessings? Do God's work. He said, "Go into the world and preach the gospel." This is for those who don't believe in Jesus Christ too. I would rather believe and receive the good part in the next life than to think I know everything now and miss the mark of going to Heaven and end up in eternal hell.

There are so many healings in my life and in many others' lives. There are just only millions of testimonies of what God has already done. Just grow up and be like the Lord Jesus Christ!

By the way, have you not been built up by His wisdom yet? I have given you the way to receive His power. I hope you find it!

But we speak the wisdom of God in a mystery, even the hidden wisdom, which God ordained before the world unto our glory. 1 Corinthians 2:7.

Dearly Beloved, I want you to hear His sweet small voice that has power to create things through YOU. Then you'll be like a son. Please continue on and get it all through Jesus! Amen.

Printed in the United States
By Bookmasters